C000062422

HELP!

I AM WALKING THROUGH TRAUMA

Katherine Bejide

Consulting Editor: Dr Jim Winter

*This booklet
is dedicated to
Andrew*

· © Day One Publications 2019
First printed 2019

ISBN 978-1-84625-641-7

Unless otherwise stated, Scripture quotations are from New
International Version (NIV) of the Holy Bible, ©2011 by Biblica

Published by Day One Publications
Ryelands Road, Leominster, HR6 8NZ
Tel 01568 613 740
North America Toll Free 888 329 6630
email—sales@dayone.co.uk
website—www.dayone.co.uk

Printed by Orchard Press Cheltenham Ltd

CONTENTS

There are very few of us who will walk through life and never be affected by trauma.

Trauma is not simply a fleeting hurt, but it is a blow to our very soul. Traumatic experiences take different forms. There is no list with a beginning and an end. They are unique experiences in which only the person involved can walk. Trauma can be one sudden experience which stops you in your tracks as it takes a sledgehammer to every aspect of your life. It can destroy, take away your breath, shatter your world and create a living nightmare. Trauma can also be dealt consistently over time through ongoing experiences, for example abuse, bullying, infertility, the breakdown of a relationship and so much more. However, trauma is always the same in one particular way. Trauma destroys, it injures, it violates and it distorts how we see the world and how we see ourselves. The fact is that we will never again be quite the same person that we were before had we never experienced it or walked with those who do.

I have written this book because I have travelled the lonely path of a traumatic experience and I have found new life through it. I want to share my story with you to encourage you. I have also written this book because being a friend or supporter of someone who is going through trauma is a difficult role to play, and I hope to be able to support and advise you too on how to go forward.

This book takes a look at my own experience of trauma and its devastating effect on my life, and how, through a very special encounter with Jesus, I was able to walk free from it: forever changed by it, but no longer clamped in its chains.

I am using the biblical story of the woman at the well in John 4 to encourage you, if you have faced trauma, that you are not alone. You are loved by a very real God who is able to pull you from the valley in which you may find yourself.

The effect of trauma can mean that Jesus may have become irrelevant to you and you have lost all belief or hope. I humbly ask you to not let that put you off reading this book. I had no time for Jesus. I dismissed him and was very angry towards him, questioning his relevance and existence. So please know that, in this book, Jesus is not a threat nor is he a religious image. He is the ultimate comforter and faithful friend, able to sit with us in darkness and yet give us light.

Each chapter contains an element of the story of 'The Woman at the Well' alongside my own story. There are no assumptions in this book and no easy answers. The aim of this book is to offer hope and support to you that there is a way through: permanently changed but with new life.

This is my interpretation of 'The Woman at the Well.' Of course, the story can be perceived in many different ways and some may find fault with my understanding of theology, historical context and interpretations. However, the beauty of this story, along with many other messages in the Bible, is that even now they can speak to us on a personal level. So it is with this story and the parallels I find reflected in my own story.

Please take your time with this book. It is a personal encounter, a space to be safe. Go at your own pace and use it as you need to.

My story

*Then the peace turned into roaring thunder
and the sky flashed with threatening light.*

*The power of the raging sea, put me in a
chokehold.*

*My body was thrown down, into the deep,
into the darkness and into the silent agony.*

Katherine Bejide

*Now [Jesus] had to go through Samaria. So
he came to a town in Samaria called Sychar,
near the plot of ground Jacob had given to his
son Joseph. Jacob's well was there, and Jesus,
tired as he was from the journey, sat down by
the well.*

(John 4:4–6)

On 15th September 2000 I had to say goodbye
to my brother. "Are you ready?" the nurse

7

asked me. I think I was breathing, I don't know. But with my friend holding me up, we walked round the longest corner there could be. Yesterday evening we had celebrated his 23rd birthday. As I had gone to bed we had bantered as siblings do. He had told me to not wake him in the morning and I had moaned at him for being a nag. The next afternoon I was told he was dead. That evening, he lay there lifeless, with a trauma to his right temple. He had a look of peace on his face and he was covered in a white sheet. The world went silent. I stood there, in some ways just as lifeless. How do you ever take that scene in? Earlier, when I had been told, I screamed, frantically looking out the window for him to come back and tell everyone to stop lying. Now, I was in silent fog.

The nurse gently ushered me up to his face. The realisation hadn't yet hit; numbness was ironically the only feeling. What was I supposed to do? Touch him? Wail? Scream? Say goodbye? How do you say goodbye to a body? How do you sum up in five minutes everything you want to say—or wish you had said? How do you acknowledge the tsunami of loss you are facing? How do you come to terms with letting go of everything you wish you had done because you thought you still had about fifty years left to do it? I got cross with him and under my breath

I whispered to him to stop messing around and to wake up. I told him I would flick his ear if he didn't.

He didn't. So I kissed him. His cold face. I told him every cliché there was in the book: that I was sorry we had argued, that I never told him enough how much I loved him. And then I walked away. Twenty-one years together and now he was gone from my life.

What I didn't realise at that moment was that, just like a Samaritan woman nearly two thousand years ago, I walked into my own deserted hideout, into the desert created by trauma. For eight years I became an outcast, not wanting anyone to help me. For eight years I pretended it didn't matter. I made choices that only laid on more shame and more guilt—endless reinforcement of my worthlessness and victim status.

Until one day, unbeknownst to me, the thirst had surfaced and I found myself walking to the well. And unbeknownst to me, someone, against the odds, was already sitting at that well and he was waiting with the greatest gift imaginable.

Rest

> *When a Samaritan woman came to draw*
> *water, Jesus said to her, 'Will you give me a*
> *drink?' (His disciples had gone into the town*
> *to buy food). The Samaritan woman said to*
> *him, 'You are a Jew and I am a Samaritan*
> *woman. How can you ask me for a drink?'*
> *(For Jews do not associate with Samaritans).*
> *(John 4:7–9)*

To go into self-defensive mode is a natural part of coping with a traumatic experience. When my brother died in a car accident, I was faced with a torrent of emotions, each wave tearing another part of me down. I couldn't make sense of what had happened or who I was anymore.

Such is the power of the event that it can be easier to not talk about it and to find a distraction from it. We simply start to survive on high alert, trying to function within a small world for fear that if we step out it may happen again.

You may be wondering who this Samaritan woman was, so I would like to take a moment to introduce you to a lady who demonstrates a path through trauma. She was an outcast from society. She had experienced abusive and traumatic relationships. She had switched off from society because she had chosen to come to the well in the middle of the afternoon (the sixth hour), a time when people do not attend the well owing to the severe heat. Her past experiences had led her into an emotional desert, a desert of loneliness and self-preservation.

But now she was faced with engagement in a conversation with Jesus who asked her for a drink. In response, she raised her shield and her defences by pointing out the barriers between them.

Jesus was beginning to challenge her defences, choosing to ignore them in spite of her protestations, choosing to meet her in the midst of her mundane life. And so we start here, with the beautiful truth that Jesus will meet you where you are right in this moment. So please stop at the well. Perhaps take the barriers down. It's just you and him. Everyone else is in town.

Encouragement for you

Prior to a traumatic experience, you may have been a fervent Christian, solid in your beliefs; or, on the other hand, Jesus may not have meant very much to you and means even less now.

When trauma is unsurfaced, we can emotionally go into self-preservation mode; it is as if an anaesthetic takes over, and one of the first things we may express is that we can no longer 'feel God'.

As time marches on, anger tends to be one of the first emotions to surface following that numbness, and much of it is directed at our nearest and dearest and at God, whether or not we had previously known him. As a Christian I have heard both believers and non-believers place the blame for their experience on God. He is the go-to when it comes to the mud-slinging. In fact, it is one of the biggest justifications today's society uses to question his existence: 'If there is a God why does he let bad things happen?'

I was not different. I had no time for God following Andrew's death. I had been very black and white in my faith; I thought it was unshakeable. It turns out that it took one devastating blow to destroy it. So do not feel guilty or ashamed if this has happened to you. It is normal and God promises not to distance himself from you because of it.

> *The Lord is close to the broken-hearted.*
> *(Psalm 34:18)*

This is a starting point, to hold on to this promise free from the pressure that you perhaps don't feel the same way about God. Hold on to it. It is truth. Truth will set you free.

However, God doesn't simply want to be close to us during our pain—he is able and desires to restore us.

> *He makes me lie down in green pastures.*
> *He leads me beside still waters.*
> *He restores my soul.*
> *(Psalm 23:2–3, ESV)*

God knows that you are consumed with your pain and unable to cope with anything but sitting with him. Restoration takes time. There is a misconception in Christianity that to praise God in our sorrows means to sing happily through gritted teeth even though we are walking through hell. The word 'praise' means to exalt. There is a song by Hillsong United called 'Even When it Hurts'. The lyrics are: 'When it hurts like hell, I'll praise you, even when it makes no sense to sing louder, then I'll sing your name.' The dictionary defines praise as 'to cry out, to place value on'. That is how we praise in our trauma—to cry out to and place value on the power of Jesus in our torment: to take his extended hand and acknowledge the value of him within a circumstance and when the waves are too big to see anything else; to invite him to sit with you whilst you rest, tired from the pain.

There is no way forward until you are able to acknowledge this distressing experience—not to explain it away but to say it matters. I do not say this lightly. This is one of the hardest things that an individual can do: to stop, to lower your shields, and to lie down.

What happened to you does not make you weak. It was not your fault and you are not a second-rate human being because of it. You are worthy of all the support, the attention and the love that you need. You are worthy of a future.

Jesus sees the heart, however broken and torn it is. He is not frightened or put off by it. He sees your pain and he feels only love. Was it coincidence that the disciples weren't at that well? Perhaps. Or perhaps this lady just needed space and time with Jesus who loved her.

There are two choices before us when we face trauma: bury it or face it and all the mess that comes with it. The former is so tempting, but it is the latter that will see us through to freedom.

There is no magic moment, there is no time when it all comes together and we have the courage or the faith levels just right. The only thing is to try and lower your resistance.

Jesus waits at the well. Sit and rest with him. Let him begin to restore you.

Encouragement for friends

> *Three of Job's friends heard of all the trouble that had fallen on him. Each travelled from his own country ... and went together to Job to keep him company and comfort him.*
> *(Job 2:11–13, The Message)*

Firstly, you are a courageous and wonderful person. So many people, when faced with a friend who is going through trauma, choose to stay away or over time they drift away. Nothing could be more damaging. It is the friends who stay the course who are truly gifts from God.

The best analogy that comes to mind of being a friend who walks with an individual through a traumatic experience is that of jumping into a rough sea in an attempt to save them from drowning. The current of trauma means that you are pulled under with them, you gasp for breath with them. Ultimately you have no control over what is happening.

As the trauma is faced, you are in a very vulnerable position. Do not be surprised if your friend changes beyond all recognition. Job's friends 'hardly recognized him' (v. 12). Do not be surprised if you are the first person in the line of fire when their pain becomes unbearable. You will have hurtful words thrown your way, you may even be blamed and you may be rejected despite having given them your time and emotional energy. It is a desperately overwhelming place to be. This can lead to a deep desire to give up or walk away. Don't.

> *They cried out in lament, ripped their robes, and dumped dirt on their heads as a sign of their grief. Then they sat with him on the ground. Seven days and nights they sat there without saying a word. They could see how rotten he felt, how deeply he was suffering.*
> *(Job 2:13, The Message)*

The most important, yet difficult, thing a friend of someone working through trauma can do is this: be consistent and expect nothing but inconsistency from them. The friendship is now weighted towards their pain and needs, and it is your love and steadfastness in the storm that will eventually help to carry them through.

Until they are ready to deal with what has happened, or if they are in the raw beginnings of the process, you do best to simply sit with them, mirror them, be their shadow and say very little. The swirl of emotions in their head do not need to be added to by well-meaning quotes, Bible verses or the search for a non-existent answer.

I will always remember the consistency and love that a friend of my mum showed in the first few days after my brother died. She would always arrive at 7 am, find where my mum was and sit next to her. She took my mum's hand and I watched as she said nothing. Nothing needed to be said. Mum just needed to be held.

By doing this we keep the way open for them to breathe in the midst of their pain and not block the way for healing. Do not hunt for answers. If they have faced abuse or persecution, do not make comments that insinuate God brought this trial to test them and help them grow. If they have lost someone, stay away from implying that God always takes the good ones. This makes him out to be cold and calculating when the Bible states the opposite.

For the first seven days after Job's devastation, his friends mirrored rest, still waters. They honoured him by handing over the control to him and didn't try to provide answers to the 'why' question.

Finally, find support just for you as you take on this supporting role. You may experience many confusing emotions. You will need a safe place to talk things through, rant and rave and perhaps deal with the original traumatic experience yourself.

> *Greater love has no one than this: to lay down one's life for one's friends.*
>
> *(John 15:13)*

The wounds matter

*Jesus answered her, 'If you knew the gift of
God and who it is that asks you for a drink,
you would have asked him and he would have
given you living water.'*

(John 4:10)

Trauma tears us apart in every way, and the damage it causes is devastating. The wound is vast and seemingly permanent. It can blow apart any healthy perception we have of ourselves. It can tear through previously held beliefs, creating sinkholes that suck away hope. It can also include physical pain. My heart physically hurt each time I heard Andrew's name. So when we are ready to acknowledge that a traumatic experience has taken place, the natural direction we then take is to look at the wounds it has created. When we do this, we are telling ourselves that we deserve healing and these wounds are not ok.

The woman at the well had her own wounds caused by broken relationships. Over years of traumatic pain and rejection, this woman had allowed her untended wounds to fester, which had altered her self-perception, particularly of her value. However, the stunning statement Jesus makes challenges this lady's view. Jesus moves the discussion to the concept of gifts. Jesus needed her to know that this living water was given with unconditional love and grace, two concepts she would find difficult to grasp. I don't think this lady had asked for much in her life. I believe that she expected nothing. To ask for anything always requires us to be vulnerable, something this lady was not willing to be.

Allowing God to take off the bandages and to look into your wounds takes trust—blind trust for some. However, dealing with your hurts starts with an acknowledgement that you are worth more than the wounds you have been left with.

Encouragement for you

The damage caused by traumatic experiences has no set pattern. It is unique to the individual and it is not for anyone else to make assumptions about the depth of pain it has caused you.

This is a very sensitive part of the booklet. Acknowledging your wounds can be between you and Jesus or with whomever you feel safe. Do not feel guilty if you are not ready: that is okay. Remember that no journey is the same. Below is simply an encouragement in ways to move forward. However, asking Jesus to show you your way is the greatest advice I can give.

If you feel that this is something you want to do, take your time. It can be an ongoing process. Sit quietly and speak to Jesus, or if you feel safer sit with a close friend and talk together. It is acknowledging that you are wounded, that the traumatic event has caused you pain. This may be all you feel you are able to do at this time, and that is fine.

As you begin to undo the dressings, I advise that you do not do this alone. Ask others to pray, to be there to support, and if necessary, ask someone who is a professional to assist you with this process. As you move forward you will need an appropriate individual there to look at the wounds and the effects they have had. The point is you don't need to have answers, you only need to have a willingness to take a look. Trauma can stop us verbally. I couldn't even say the word 'Andrew' for a long time. There may be people who have caused you trauma and even stating their names can be its own mountain. That's ok.

You are still at rest with Jesus and he is with you. There is no schedule.

Trauma can lead to maladaptive choices. It was not until I had removed layers of my pain that I came to look at a hidden wound, where I identified a particular hurt that a lot of my choices had been based on. The choices weren't directly linked to Andrew's death, but rather to a certain part of it that had subsequently twisted my perception of self-worth. That wound and that rot had led me to strive to create a sense of my own worth in relationships.

God wants us to let him see our wound. The truth is, the only way to heal the wound is to expose it. Our loving God weeps at seeing your pain and his heart breaks like any parent at seeing what that pain has done to you.

> *He gives strength to the weary and increases*
> *the power of the weak.*
>
> *(Isaiah 40:29)*

Encouragement for friends

> *A man of many companions may come to*
> *ruin, but there is a friend who sticks closer*
> *than a brother.* *(Proverbs 18:24, ESV)*

In order to walk with friends who have faced a traumatic experience, you need to freely give of yourself with no expectations. However, when they begin to address their wounds, be there to give them hope and encouragement. Both can lead to you upholding their value whilst they cannot feel it for themselves at that time.

> *When Moses' hands grew tired, they took a stone and put it under him and he sat on it. Aaron and Hur held his hands up—one on one side, one on the other—so that his hands remained steady till sunset.*
>
> *(Exodus 17:12)*

Trauma leaves us broken. In the above biblical scenario we witness a man of faith, Moses, growing weary. He needed his friends to stand with him. They held his hands and kept steady. It is this that we as friends are required to do.

When a soldier is wounded on a battlefield, comrades will look to shield their friend whilst they await rescue. They acknowledge what has happened and they take the wounds seriously. I have heard people say to those in trauma that time doesn't heal and it never gets any better. This is not true, and words like this mean we may as well snuff the breath out of them ourselves. No, a comrade will speak comfort and words of hope that things will be ok, that there is life. They hold them if necessary, allow them to shout out in the pain or their fear, and let them talk. They champion life and channel hope as they hold their hand in the fear and the uncertainty.

> *Surely he will save you from the fowler's snare*
> *and from the deadly pestilence.*
> *He will cover you with his feathers,*
> *and under his wings you will find refuge;*
> *his faithfulness will be your shield and rampart.*
> *You will not fear the terror of night,*
> *nor the arrow that flies by day.*
>
> *(Psalm 91:3–5)*

If we are to be Christ-like in our interactions then the verse above clarifies how we deal with the wounds of a loved one. We are to be a refuge not a doctor. We are called to shield them from the terror that this event has caused and to be a rampart when the arrows of fear look to wound further.

We must not treat them differently. This does not mean pretending the trauma does not exist; it means that love doesn't change. We tend to avoid people when an uncomfortable topic is brought up. We might become awkward if they disclose that they were abused, or we may not know what to say if our friend tells us they are struggling to conceive. Perhaps they are going through a divorce that divides our loyalty, or they have faced religious abuse that we can't connect with and so avoid the topic of God altogether. Perhaps they are grieving so we don't mention the loved one's name. Whatever the event was, the vastness and magnitude of it can make us treat them with kid gloves or try to pretend that it never happened and carry on as before. This is not your role and can lead to your friend feeling ever so alone and frightened.

So, on a practical level, how do we address wounds? We adapt.

We see in the Bible many occasions where Jesus adapted to a wounded individual's situation. He stopped to speak to the woman who bled; he attended the house of grieving parents; he spoke with the leper; and he was interrupted by a paraplegic man being lowered through a roof in need of healing. Jesus was constantly adapting to people's wounds.

By adapting and being able to meet them just where they are at in that day, we are creating a safe place.

When I returned to work following the death of my brother, I returned a wounded mess. I needed my friends to provide a safe house for me, to be themselves within my situation, not to try to make me who they wanted me to be in their situation.

Some pretended that it hadn't happened and carried on. This led to fear. However, others adapted themselves and made me feel safe and as normal as they could. One told me that he just wanted to be whatever I needed him to be, whether to talk about it or not. He was ready to adapt. Another friend was always at the end of a text message available with a hug, and another offered to go to work with me because they knew that was a time (especially on a crowded train) where I would feel vulnerable and frightened. These individuals knew they were holding a wounded friend. They were shields.

So be prepared to adapt. It can be frustrating and it can be a long journey. Never concern yourself with worries of being overly 'there'. I have never once heard someone facing trauma claim that someone is caring too much. Take your cue from them and unless they tell you to ease off, then keep going. Be consistent and be in it for the duration. Be a safe place.

Caves and mountains

'Sir,' the woman said, 'you have nothing to draw with and the well is deep. Where can you get this living water? Are you greater than our father Jacob, who gave us the well and drank from it himself, as did also his sons and his livestock?'

Jesus answered, 'Everyone who drinks this water will be thirsty again, but whoever drinks the water I give them will never thirst. Indeed, the water I give them will become in them a spring of water welling up to eternal life.'

(John 4:11–14)

Victimhood is a very real issue. We become comfortable with believing that because something bad has happened to us, then all things that happen from that point on will be bad. Life almost becomes a self-fulfilling prophecy as we look for new traumatic events. Following a traumatic experience, I have often heard individuals talking about themselves as being a victim. They carry their brokenness, defining themselves through what has occurred. I do not take away the meaningfulness of this step, as we must acknowledge we are in fact victims of deeply painful circumstances. It is a justified question to ask 'why me?' The problem with this is that, unless we can let go of this question, we risk becoming stuck in our pain.

I do not believe being a victim of an event is where our journey ends.

Jesus had previously spoken to the woman at the well about his gift that would allow her to have life. Following his astonishing offer, the natural response would be to 'tell me more'. However, this lady dismisses the depth of what he is saying. She is comfortable with living in the shadow of her broken identity. She is determined to look at the impossibility of his statement, stating that 'he has nothing to use' and 'it is too deep'. This well has served a purpose. It has been effective and done what it should do. It has served not only this woman but also many generations of people and livestock, all the way back to Jacob and his sons. It is historical.

This lady has pitched her tent and built her walls around it. How? Through the subsequent choices that have been made since becoming a victim of trauma. She believes in her role as a victim and an outcast and makes a direct comparison between Jesus and what she already has to satisfy her thirst.

Strategies that distract us from our experience bury and bind us. The problem with burying pain is the need to keep on burying it. We give these coping mechanisms power and bind ourselves to them, but inevitably they cannot sustain us. The list is endless. For me it was bad relationships, negative self-talk and excessive drinking. When they leave us, or are no longer effective, then that adds another layer of pain, rejection, heartache and emptiness. The cycle begins again as we look to the next thing. These layers set like cement, burying the real wound further and further down and creating walls around us.

Encouragement for you

I'm hurt and in pain, give me space for
healing, and mountain air.
(Psalm 69:20, The Message)

Trauma leaves us feeling helpless. This is inevitable. Our world has been ripped apart, distorted and has taken a turn that it shouldn't have. It leads us to feeling as though we have no control. The world is a frightening place so we withdraw.

It is easy to metaphorically slink into a cave when we have faced pain. It can make us feel protected and invisible. To put even a little bit of you into the sunlight feels far too exposed. Of course there is a time when the world may become smaller. Following Andrew's death our home was our base and to go outside and function took time. There is no shame in taking time whilst you process what has happened—to shut down, close the doors and only allow those who make you feel safe to come close. But I do not believe that this is your destination point.

Elijah was a prophet from the Old Testament. He was a man of God, used powerfully to speak words on God's behalf. However, as for many of us, there was a time when trauma loomed, and with it came fear and a strong sense of vulnerability. Elijah was threatened with assassination. Even though he was held aloft by God's people, trauma made him run; his identity in his God had come second to victimhood.

However, God still searched for him.

And the word of the LORD came to him:
'What are you doing here, Elijah?'

He replied, 'I have been very zealous for
the LORD God Almighty. The Israelites have
rejected your covenant, torn down your altars,
and put your prophets to death with the
sword. I am the only one left, and now they
are trying to kill me too.'

The LORD said, 'Go out and stand on the
mountain in the presence of the LORD, for the
LORD is about to pass by.'

(1 Kings 19:9-11)

God of course knew why Elijah was in a cave on
the mountainside. It was providing a false shelter,
even though Elijah considered it a safe place.
However, God considered it purposeless. So, despite
the pain and the fear, he told him to go and stand
on the mountain, but in the presence of the Lord.
The presence of the Lord was the only protection
he needed.

Caves and mountains are the exact opposite of one
another: one hides, the other exposes; one allows us
to see all that is in front of us, the other means we
can only ruminate on what has been; one means
we have to run in, the other means that we have to
climb up. There is no life in a cave—there is only
existence. A mountain top provides a view of all the

eye can see. It sets our sights higher than where we are in that moment. There is no life in victimhood— only existence. The darkness is only allowing you to see shadows.

Never is there more explicit clarification in the Bible about the purpose of Jesus Christ than this:

> *The thief comes only to steal and kill and*
> *destroy; I have come that they may have life,*
> *and have it to the full.*
>
> *(John 10:10)*

This statement is absolute. It does not end with a condition that you will only have life if nothing bad happens along the way. No, Jesus offers fullness of life to you. Simple survival is not your portion.

For eight years, I perceived the death of my brother as being a wave that threw me off course. In my mind I thought that had it not happened, I would have fulfilled my purpose in life. I was sitting in a metaphorical cave staring at walls and ruminating on what could have been. In doing so, I was ignoring the gaping exit into the light. I have often heard people who have faced trauma describing their future as now being on a second-rate path. There is no second-rate path because you are not second-rate. Oh yes, life has changed beyond recognition and it isn't ever going to be the same. However, it can be just as beautiful when you are ready to grasp it again. We live in the realm of looking backwards and forwards. God lives in the realm of restoration and redemption. I do not intend to take away from the damage that the experience caused, not at all. I simply want you to realise that you still have life ahead of you—life to the full.

> *Then a great and powerful wind tore the*
> *mountains apart and shattered the rocks*
> *before the* LORD, *but the* LORD *was not*
> *in the wind. After the wind there was an*
> *earthquake, but the* LORD *was not in the*
> *earthquake. After the earthquake came a fire,*
> *but the* LORD *was not in the fire. And after*
> *the fire came a gentle whisper. When Elijah*
> *heard it, he pulled his cloak over his face and*
> *went out and stood at the mouth of the cave.*
> *(1 Kings 19:11–13)*

God knows you are frightened. He knows that to step out into life again, a life that looks totally different from what it would have been and has left you acutely aware that it can hurt you, is terrifying.

He comes to you with a gentle whisper. Not a loud and unnerving earthquake, and not a fire that alarms and is unapproachable. No, a gentle whisper as he passes by. It is the whisper that motivated Elijah to stand at the mouth of the cave.

And that is the essence of the challenge that we face today. To deal with things effectively and thoroughly takes courage. We need to put aside the strategies that we have used to build up an identity which keeps us chained to our trauma. It means being raw, vulnerable and honest. It means to stare into the eye of the storm and sit with the pain, the heartache and the emotions that come with it. It means to return sometimes to that place of pain because it is the only way that restoration will truly be able to come.

It might be that you want to step out but need reassurance. Lean into the friendships that give you this. Be open to your friends' advice. They may be outside of the cave. They can tell you it is safe. They can help you come forward. They can help you to walk out.

You are not destined to be a victim.

Encouragement for friends

A friend loves at all times,
and a brother is born for a time of adversity.
(Proverbs 17:17)

Earlier I touched on the idea that encouragement needs to play a crucial role in walking with a friend who has faced trauma. This experience will change them. You may be able to recognise strategies, behaviours or actions that mean they are heading into a cave or loitering at the entrance. You will not have any control of their choices. Whilst the love you hold will want them to be free, it is a gruelling and patient task to allow them to sit in their cave.

Encouragement empowers as it can directly break through lies. It doesn't mean we pop up every so often in their lives with a cryptic poem about empowerment or look to tell them they are fine when they are not. Encouragement is a deep and powerful gift that can move mountains within a person's life.

Encouragement means to support. When and why do individuals need support? When they are not capable of doing something by themselves. Support is not taking over. Essentially, it is to help them carry their load and give them the strength to see it through. However, how do we do this when they have found their cave?

We allow them to speak freely. I spent many hours being supported by friends who would just listen. These conversations weren't about Andrew dying, as we know I wasn't in a place to acknowledge this had happened. Most of the time it was about another damaging decision I had made, which at the time I just saw as life. I couldn't understand why I kept hitting the same problems, mainly because I was limited by the cave walls that I had surrounded myself with! But here is the crux of it. My friends could have run out of patience and told me all these issues were down to the cave I had chosen to put myself in. They could have walked away, but they didn't. They let me talk and they took every problem I had seriously. In this way I felt supported. I was asking for someone to come and sit with me in there, not to drag me out but just to listen. They propped me up, they took me seriously and they didn't push.

To support a friend through the onslaught of emotions that come with facing a trauma can be frightening and overwhelming. They are unpredictable and inconsistent. One moment they can be feeling positive, and the next, extremely negative. Be prepared for this and ask God to give you the grace and strength to help them through these moments. I will never forget two particular occasions where I went from relatively calm to all of a sudden sobbing over Andrew. The two people physically closest to me on these occasions wrapped their arms around me, said nothing and allowed me to sob. Those arms held me so closely and allowed me to feel held up in my vulnerability.

When someone is walking through trauma and the subsequent pain, they are in a vulnerable position where confidence needs to be rebuilt as it is easily knocked down or may even be non-existent. One reason for this is because when an individual is looking to feel safe again, they can put their trust and their strength into things that make them feel validated and worth something. Ultimately these things will let them down. When they do, the validation is knocked, and the confidence goes too. Encouragement from a consistent friend will allow your friend to feel supported, even when they make choices you don't agree with because you see them being let down. If you stay consistent, you are acting as a safe buffer, a buffer that will begin to make them realise that there are safe places and safe people in this world.

I spent many years not truly seeing the worth of faithful friends. I would be fully fixated on the 'thing' that was acting as my cave, trying to keep it around me. I didn't have much time for people who weren't connected to it; however, one thing I did know, they were there and I could call them. I could meet them for a coffee and talk for hours if I needed to. I look back now and I see them with such different eyes. What amazing people who I wish I had valued more. I can't name them all—I wish I could—but I thank them here and now for the support and the consistent encouragement they showed. How did they do this? By being there. By telling me even when I didn't want to hear it that I meant something. By inviting me to everything going even when, let's be honest, I was at best unpredictable company!

Try not to be frustrated with your friend when they are more concerned with things that you can see are not the way forward. It's hard, and of course as a friend you must be graciously honest, but don't be surprised if they don't want to hear it. Keep letting them come back to you, keep supporting them. It is an issue of confidence, and your encouragement is allowing it to grow. Eventually you might realise that they have joined you at the entrance to their cave.

Mountain air

You are precious ... and ... I love you.
(Isaiah 43:4)

What follows in this chapter is the turning point in my walk. No healing process is ever the same, but this is to encourage you that all I have written leads somewhere.

We have come to the point in the chapter when the woman at the well begins to focus on freedom more than on her trauma: 'Sir, give me this water so that I won't get thirsty and have to keep coming here to draw water' (John 4:15).

She sees the cave exit. She is admitting that the water she currently uses is not satisfying her thirst and the cave is not where she wants to be. She is yearning for life. The dialogue between Jesus and the woman at the well has been an awkward conversation. Jesus isn't looking for a perfect chat; he will meet us where we are for however long, knowing the complexity and mess involved with trauma and its impact on the human heart.

Admitting to God that I needed him to break in was much like the conversation that this woman had with Jesus—clumsy and stop-start in nature—and it lasted for eight years. It was not a quick fix.

In 2008, I had gone to a church camp because I saw it as a social event. I had made a deal with myself just to be on the outskirts. The first evening, whilst everyone else was in a meeting, I walked around the site, creating my own familiar desert.

A couple of evenings in, I was walking back to my tent and in the stillness of the night I felt a whisper in my spirit: 'Will you give me a moment?' My normal response would have been to shrug this request off, but it caught me off guard. For some reason in that fleeting moment, I trusted and whispered 'yes'.

The next morning my friends encouraged me to attend just one meeting. With disdain I agreed.

As the meeting got started, the same question that had been whispered to me the evening before was being whispered to me again: 'Will you give me a drink?' It was followed by a feeling in my heart that I had had enough of this exhausting journey.

The morning speaker introduced himself and then he told us that he had been asked to preach on one verse in the Bible. The verse was: 'Jesus wept' (John 11:35). He carried on, 'For today I would like to link this verse to one thing. I want to talk about this Bible verse in the context of when we lose someone we love, when we are faced with grief.'

'Oh my God,' I whispered as my tears broke through.

As the preacher spoke about God's heart in grief and trauma, every single statement was like a hammer chipping away at the strongholds I had built over my life. However, the breakthrough came when I finally realised that God found no joy or purpose in Andrew's death. God had wept with me and held me; he was angry; he didn't want this for me, and above all, he knew more than anyone else the depth of pain I had walked with.

Eight years of pain was coming out, and as it did, he spoke:

> *I know that every choice you have made*
> *has been to stem the pain of losing Andrew.*
> *I know that you have hurt yourself to try*
> *and get rid of the grief. I wanted to get rid*
> *of it for you. I have seen the heart-broken*
> *tears you have cried. I sat there and cried*
> *them with you. I know that every drink*

41

you have had and every relationship you
have entered into was simply a reflection of
the way you see yourself since losing him.
I know because I have yearned for you to
see yourself how I see you. I am your friend,
I am your healer and I am your Dad. In this
moment be free from the chains.

I was listening to God's heartbeat. It beat for me. There is always a moment in dealing with the traumatic experience that we have to face the root cause. The moment when we have to look directly into the eye of the storm. God had to get me to the point where I could stare into the face of my loss and stand up in the midst of it because his presence was holding me up.

And so it is with our woman at the well. It has reached the point where she needs to face her pain. Jesus tells her, 'Go, call your husband and come back.' Asking this lady to bring her husband seemed such an 'off-the-topic' request, catching her off guard. I feel this lady's vulnerability in her response as she replies, 'I have no husband.' I almost feel her thinking, 'Why would he bring that up? Why would he hurt me like that?' However, Jesus doesn't stop there, he needs to go further, so he says to her, 'You are right when you say you have no husband. The fact is, you have had five husbands, and the man you now have is not your husband. What you have just said is quite true' (John 4:16–18). I believe that Jesus was about to create beauty from brokenness, and to allow her to stare into the eye of her storm. Her crushed heart and spirit was about to have life poured into it.

There was no judgement in Jesus' voice when he told her that he knew. He knew that she had had five husbands. There was no 'but'. He simply stopped after he had pointed out that he knew. There is one thing Jesus was trying to do in this moment with the Samaritan woman, and in the moment with me. He wanted us to know that we are loved and worth just as much as we had ever been. He knew it all.

When we face immense pain in our life, there can be well-meaning attempts by others to try to put themselves in our shoes. They may say that they know how we feel, or they may just make comments that imply that they understand our pain. Sadly, for those who are facing the pain, regardless of how buried or conscious of it they are, there is nothing lonelier than facing trauma. For people don't know. Even those who have faced something similar and can show understanding are not the ones walking in their shoes, shutting the door at night, waking up, remembering the next morning and having to start the cycle over again. We do not know, we can only walk with them. However, there is one who does know. One who not only knows but also feels it with you. And unlike our strategies, he can heal, restore and make the sun rise again.

The speaker gently asked everyone in the congregation to stand up. He did this because he knew the level of vulnerability some of us were feeling. He asked everyone to close their eyes and he spoke. He spoke of those who had lost someone and how they were stuck in their grief. He told us that God wanted to unstick us today, that we didn't need to stay where we were. Then he asked us, if we wanted to be free, to raise our hands. This was not an easy thing to do. This was letting go of eight years of identity, choices, self-held beliefs and strategies. This was laying it all down.

With my head looking downward, my hand moved slowly away from my face where it had hopelessly tried to catch the tears that were coming so fast and so powerfully, I could barely stem the noise of sobbing. They had taken me by surprise, they were coming from my very soul: 'deep had cried to deep' (Psalm 42:7). When the congregation was asked to see if anyone around them had their hand raised, I felt a multitude of hands rest on me and pray. Then a woman came over. We sat together and I did something that I had needed to do for eight years. I admitted that I was angry. I was so angry that Andrew had died. I was angry that everyone else had their siblings and that I had had to go through this. I felt the rage as we spoke, and I did not hold back in how loudly I was telling this wonderful woman about the depth of anger that I was feeling. We sat together and we prayed. She prayed that the anger, as relevant and ok as it was, would now be gone that the heart would be healed. And she proclaimed over me that this broken heart that I had faced for eight years was no longer broken. From that moment on, the physical heartbreak that had come whenever people talked about Andrew never returned.

Then I knew—I had to let him go. I had never really known what 'letting go' meant. The concept would make me angry because there was never going to be a day when I could forget what had happened. Truly, I do not believe that is what it means to let go.

Trauma is a monster. It will grasp you by the shoulders and hold you against a wall of pain for as long as it is able. Letting go is to have the courage to take its hands from around your neck and be released from its grip. I had to let go of making my tragedy my identity.

I needed Jesus to breathe into me a new identity. And as I sat in my chair, I felt something happen. Not a ghost-like experience, but one that reflected that Jesus has conquered death and love never ends. I felt Jesus come and sit to the left of me, and I felt Andrew sitting at the right. I told Andrew I was going to let him go, and as I did, I felt him go. Not the love, never the love, but the need to tie my life to his death. Andrew is at peace and I will see him again one day. In the meantime, there is a life and purpose to fulfil. From that day, my heart never physically hurt again.

Jesus went nowhere. Jesus stayed.

However, there was also eight years of damage to my perception of Jesus. Our relationship was something I had walked away from. One of the biggest lies that I had to overcome was the belief that God had personally killed my brother and that he was indifferent to my suffering. Why hadn't he stopped the lorry? Why had he let it happen?

There needed to be a letting go of these lies and questions to move forward.

The damage trauma can do to our relationship with God or our concept of Christ is immense and it begins with the feeling of being forsaken.

Encouragement

For this part, I have merged encouragement both for those walking the path of pain, and for those walking alongside them. I have done this because, for both, there can be a feeling of being forsaken and consequently there can be misguided perceptions about Christ.

As the person experiencing the pain of trauma, your level of feeling forsaken is substantial and I am not trying to equate the feelings of those around you with your own. However, having looked with hindsight on the journey that my friends walked at the time my brother died, I believe that the 'friend' can feel forsaken too. When a friend faces distress through varying degrees of trauma, they inevitably change, they can close off from us, they might head to other people who they think can understand more than we do, leaving us feeling empty.

To be forsaken is to be 'abandoned or deserted'.

In the midst of my search for answers, I attended a prayer session run by a London convent. Whilst there, one of the ladies who I sat beside told me something that at that time made no sense to me: 'God wants you to know that he has allowed you to carry a piece of his cross.'

This seems an incredibly insensitive statement. I do not advocate using it with anyone you are walking alongside at the moment; neither, if you are reading this in pain, would I say this without explaining myself. I felt only resentment towards her statement. I didn't ask to carry his cross—I had no choice.

To fully understand what she meant, we have to look more closely at the cross.

Prior to the cross being a symbol of new life, it represented an agonising death. It was a way to be turned into an exhibit whilst you felt the oxygen leaving your body for the last time. For Jesus, it was symbolic of injustice, betrayal and painful wrongdoing; all such words may resonate with you.

Jesus knew what it was like to be faced with every tormenting emotion known to the human soul. He stood alone. Jesus faced death in front of the people whom he had come to love and save. Jesus faced rejection from these people to whom he had shown only love, whom he had healed, sat with and stood up for. They bullied him, they tortured him, and they degraded him. Jesus had to cling on to his relationship with his Father by the very skin of his teeth. As he hung there, he cried out to his Father, *'Eli, Eli, lema sabachthani?'* (which means 'My God, my God, why have you forsaken me?') (Matthew 27:46).

Yet, in our own pain, we are still tempted to believe that he doesn't know what we are going through.

Jesus knows exactly what we are going through. We know this because there is no greater representation of trauma than the cross.

Trauma makes us desperate. A few days into my grief, I remember slumping on to a swing in the local park, sobbing. I was completely lost, alone and frightened. As I sobbed I closed my eyes and I implored God to take it from me, begging that when I opened my eyes it would have all been a nightmare and that Andrew would be at home. I never wanted to open my eyes again.

Jesus begged for it to be taken from him too.

> *He withdrew about a stone's throw beyond*
> *them, knelt down and prayed, 'Father, if you*
> *are willing, take this cup from me; yet not my*
> *will, but yours be done.'*
>
> *(Luke 22:41–42)*

There is a danger that we read verses like this and picture Jesus in a serene state, not shaken or frightened by what is about to happen but declaring God's will be done. So let's be clear.

*And being in anguish, he prayed more
earnestly, and his sweat was like drops of
blood falling to the ground.*

(*Luke 22:44*)

These words were said with emotion, through tears and gritted teeth, and perhaps he shook as he shouted or whispered them out.

And the reality of trauma is just that: at some point we have to open our eyes, because just as there was no choice for Jesus, there is no choice and no way out for us. We can only face it where we are at today and in this moment. This happened to you and you had no control over it. That means that you have had to walk a path with your cross just as Jesus had to walk from Jerusalem to Calvary.

*As the soldiers led him away, they seized
Simon from Cyrene, who was on his way in
from the country, and put the cross on him
and made him carry it behind Jesus.*

(*Luke 23:26*)

Simon was on his way in from the country, which infers that he wasn't part of the baying mob surrounding Jesus. However, they 'seized' him and made him carry the cross for Jesus. He did not volunteer. He may have felt victimized, 'Why not the man next to me?' 'Why me?' In one moment he felt the weight of trauma.

The day that Andrew died, my family were pulled from the crowd, pushed to the ground and made to carry the cross. We were seized by fear, panic, loneliness, and many other overwhelming and unpredictable emotions. In the same way it was you who were pushed down to the ground with Jesus. Why you? I don't know. Why me? I don't know.

However, there must be a point in the story when the cross moves from being a symbol of hopelessness to a feeling of hope. It is the moment we were able to hand it back to Jesus.

Although it is not biblically documented, there must have come a point when Simon let go of the cross.

Imagine, if you will, a moment when he lifted that ugly, heavy and scathing wooden cross and placed it onto the back of Jesus. I should imagine a part of him was reluctant, and another part relieved, but Simon would have been forever changed.

Every individual who has been asked to carry the cross for Jesus comes to a point in their journey when they have to hand it back if they want resolution and reconciliation. However, even in doing this, you will not be the same as you were beforehand. Firstly, you will have scars that you will carry with you for the rest of your life. The very experience that you have suffered will stay with you forever. Nevertheless, you are able to stand again, and you are able to live a full and beautiful life again should you so choose. Why? Because Jesus will take it from you and in return place new life into your hands.

Good Friday starkly demonstrates the devastation caused by trauma, the pain and the wounds, the confusion that makes life a fog and an existence alongside the 'what now?' question. For the friends of those in pain, it is a reflection of helplessness, of 'what ifs'. The night draws on, and the darkness brings with it irrational thought, desperation and fear. This is the time when we need to trust, to allow faith to rise. We need to hold on to the promise Jesus gave us that 'it is finished'.

Then the sun rises on Easter Sunday: it rises on restoration and redemption as Jesus' disciples see that he has risen. He appears before them. He has conquered death. There is hope.

'Peace be with you,' Jesus says to his disciples and to us (Luke 24:36).

This is the crux of what this lady was telling me about carrying Christ's cross, and this is the crux of what I want to tell you—your cross is Jesus' cross, and because he loves you he wants to take it from you.

When you allow him to, from your pain there will come purpose. There can be purpose from trauma. It may feel like there was no purpose in what happened to you, but redemption through Jesus can turn it into a powerful tool for good.

God your Father will give you everything you need to be not only sustained, but also to move into the hope and the promises that are yours. Yes, you carried the cross with him and that was powerful, but now you can hand it back and you can be empowered, freed from fear and looking forward to the purposes that he can bring from your pain.

Jesus is not indifferent to your pain. He is wanting to take your pain, your cross and make it into something new.

There is something more powerful and life-changing than trauma, and that is the love and power of Jesus Christ.

A new identity

*'Sir,' the woman said, 'I can see that you are
a prophet. Our ancestors worshipped on this
mountain, but you Jews claim that the place
where we must worship is in Jerusalem.'*
(John 4:19–20)

A traumatic experience will forever change us.
We know this. Sometimes it can feel as though
we are living a secondary existence. However,
dare I suggest that this change may end up being
just as beautiful a life had it not happened? Am I
suggesting that it is a good thing that your trauma
occurred? Absolutely not. I miss my brother every
day. I would give so much to have him with me
and there will always be fresh hurts around his
death. What I am putting forward is the suggestion
that through healing, life can be just as beautiful
and magnificent as the life you would have had
without it.

These verses create a change in the tone of their conversation. It is unclear as to why, but I believe that the woman is touching on the topic of identity. By pointing to the legalistic conflicts between Jews and Samaritans, she has emphasised the divide between herself and Jesus, perhaps suggesting that who she is will not fit in with who she assumes he wants her to be. So she hesitates at drawing closer.

But this lady had never encountered salvation until now.

> 'Woman,' Jesus replied, 'believe me, a time is coming when you will worship the Father neither on this mountain nor in Jerusalem. You Samaritans worship what you do not know; we worship what we do know, for salvation is from the Jews.'
>
> (John 4:21–22)

Salvation means 'the act of saving or protecting from harm, risk, loss or destruction'. Jesus wanted this woman at the well to know he was the ultimate Saviour; he wants you to know he is the ultimate Saviour. Jesus sets out who he is and that is non-negotiable.

Had it not been for Jesus at my well, I would not have experienced his deep love and the transformation in my life that has led me to where I am today. I say 'transformation' with caution. Jesus didn't change me into a person I am not. He gave me life that has allowed me to break free from my chains; he has shown me my value and my purpose; he transformed me from a tired, hardened, pain-filled individual who only believed in shame and the scraps of life being mine, into a woman who embraces her worth, life's joy and views life from the mountain top.

In many incidents in the Bible, when people encounter Jesus, he takes time to converse with them, and in varying ways he reveals his love for them. Then there is a shock for the recipient when he chooses them to speak to, or defends them against, the baying mob. There are public encounters, private encounters, shock encounters and much-desired encounters; however, they all have the same theme: love, acceptance, the realisation of worth; and then a desire, not a forced choice, to make the changes necessary to be free.

With pain come habits, beliefs and a way of life. Depending on how long we have faced the pain will determine how heavy and ingrained these habits are. Earlier, we spoke about strategies and coping mechanisms. These create the strongholds in our lives and move us away from knowing Jesus. These are the kinds of things that Jesus wants to free us from.

When we experience a true encounter with Jesus, it may not be that our habits break automatically. For me it took a while, for the simple reason that they were habits. However, the key thing was this: they no longer worked; they made me unhappy and I wanted to be rid of them.

Jesus doesn't have a 'one-mould-fits-all-Christian'. He is not looking to fit you into a mould. No, he is looking to be your salvation from the things in your life that limit you and cause you pain and ultimately block the way to having a relationship with him. He is looking to give you his living water to replace the water that you have chosen.

> *Yet a time is coming and has now come when the true worshippers will worship the Father in the Spirit and in truth, for they are the kind of worshippers the Father seeks. God is spirit, and his worshippers must worship in the Spirit and in truth.*
>
> *(John 4:23–24)*

This is not about: 'Had Andrew not died I would not have become who I am.' That's trite.

No, this is about: 'Had I not experienced the powerful healing of Jesus Christ I would not have become who I am now.'

Encouragement for you

There is a verse in the Bible that says: 'And we know that in all things God works for the good of those who love him' (Romans 8:28). This is a dangerous Bible verse which I believe is used too often and used inappropriately when speaking to those facing pain and anguish. For some reason it is a 'go to' passage when needing to provide an answer. Please know that people may not want to hear that Bible verse when they are under the shadow of trauma.

However, looked at from a different perspective, this is the essence of salvation. God wants not only to bring you through your pain, but also to work for your good and bring to life a new spirit and a new truth. Your experience hurts and angers him and it will never be a beautiful thing; but he is bigger and is able to take your cross and hand you beauty instead.

If, when we experience healing, we shed an old identity, then surely we have to build a new one. We have been set free, reborn almost, and we have moved away from living the victim lifestyle. However, we still have a day-to-day life which is the same as it has always been. So how does it work to be a new creation?

God will not leave you empty, neither does he expect you to go back to the person you were before you faced trauma. In order to reach the mountain-top, we must climb. However, he has equipped us with every blessing, giving the ability to reach the peak. You will not find your new self in one go. Life is a journey. What God has done is equip you with every blessing.

It may be that since you began reading this book you are perhaps opening up to the idea of acknowledging what has happened in your life, or even the possibility of healing. This is your personal journey in your time. It does not all come together in one moment. Now is the beginning of a journey where God will reveal to you his plans and the adventure that he has in store for you.

The road to Damascus is one of the more well-known stories in the Bible (Acts 9). It tells the story of a powerful man called Saul, who hated Christians. He would have them stoned and would do anything within his power to eradicate them from the earth.

Saul had an encounter with Jesus Christ whereby he was blinded. After time with one of Jesus' followers he was able to see again as the scales fell from his eyes. He was later renamed Paul and the old identity of Saul was forgotten.

The reason I tell this story is that after the scales fell from his eyes Paul, in preparation for his further ministry, spent approximately three years in Arabia, wisely spending time reflecting, learning new ways and unlearning old ways. He had to change his mindset through learning about 'The Word'. He took time to 'be'.

May I suggest that as you come into this new hope, you do the same? Take time to get to know the true Jesus Christ, not the one you have held at arm's length. There will be parts of you that need to be uncovered, ways of thinking that need to be unlearned, perhaps dreams and goals that you had forgotten about.

New adventures are going to be opened up, old dreams are going to have life breathed into them again. Old habits will need time to be broken and perhaps friendships might need to be healed. This is an exciting time, so take it for you. You were not brought into new life to be given an agenda. You were given new life because you're loved by a very real God.

> *May the God of hope fill you with all joy and peace as you trust in him, so that you may overflow with hope by the power of the Holy Spirit.*
>
> *(Romans 15:13)*

Encouragement for friends

It might be that you are currently walking with someone who is carving out a new identity following a painful experience. This is not a simple process and can be fraught with twists and turns. It is essential that you give them the support to find it. The most tempting thing you as a friend may want to do is tell them what they should be doing. If you are watching them make bad choices that they would never have made before, the most damaging line that can come out of your mouth is: 'You need to...'

It is easy for us to want to challenge them—that will make them feel judged. It is easy for us to want to point out what we are witnessing—that will make them feel like a freak. Your friend is frightened; your friend is lost. Dare I suggest that if you were walking the path they are, your choices might not always be as clear cut as you think they would be. It is a frustrating yet obvious thing that you must do. Tag along. They might get it hugely wrong sometimes. You simply cannot imagine what they are going through even if you have faced the same thing. Our feelings are as unique as our fingerprints.

I have very nearly blasted off my opinion in the past when I have seen friends who are in pain making life choices that I didn't agree with. What stops me? The fact that regardless of whether my opinion is right or wrong, I am not living their hell, I do not understand what they are going through and therefore my advice is heavily tilted towards a reality that they are not living in. Sometimes we want them to handle it how their old self would. But they are not their old self. They don't know who they are anymore. You must leave the way open for them to move forward into their new Christ-given identity.

All that people want and can handle in the valley is other people walking with them. So do that. You don't have to agree with them. They may annoy you, deeply frustrate you and there will be times when you want to give up on them. Please don't, just keep your thoughts to yourself and your hand open for them to grab. Let them know you are there for coffee. Keep sending love. Importantly, expect nothing back. Sometimes they will respond, but don't take it personally when they don't. It is you who needs to remain consistent. Will you sometimes say the wrong thing? Yes. Will they sometimes say the wrong thing? Yes. Will you face rejection and anger? Yes.

Are you prepared to stay as they courageously work things through?

Hang in there. It might be your hand that is stopping them from falling.

Final thoughts

*The woman said, 'I know that Messiah'
(called Christ) 'is coming. When he comes he
will explain everything to us.'*
  *Then Jesus declared, 'I, the one speaking to
you—I am he.'*

  (John 4:25–26)

Encounters can be powerful things: they reveal moments to us, things that we didn't know about ourselves. They can blow our minds, and crucially, they hold the door open for us to walk in to fresh hope and new life, to let go and grasp newness.

*Then, leaving her water jar, the woman
went back to the town and said to the people,
'Come, see a man who told me everything
I ever did. Could this be the Messiah?'*
  (John 4:28–29)

The woman had come to the well expecting only to collect her water and then leave. We don't know how long this conversation had gone on for. However, it was powerful. She had gone from reaction, to response, to engagement. She had engaged in discussion and for fleeting moments felt levels of acceptance she would have not experienced in a long time, if ever. The Bible says that she left her water jar. Of course, I am speaking symbolically and could be accused of reading too much into this. But, the Samaritan woman left behind what encapsulated her function, her cave, her worth, her need, her life-line, to go back into town to the place that she had wanted to avoid. There is a letting go that is occurring here.

I talked about the concept of letting go when I allowed God to pass by. We must let go of 'why me'? There is no answer to this question.

By letting go of her water jar, this women is demonstrating the worth that Jesus had placed within her from this encounter. There was no fear, only courage as a result of the lies being banished, and she was dancing in the healing rain and the living water of Jesus. She had found truth.

Jars are cumbersome items. When they are full, we tend to have to carry them with both hands whilst we focus on not spilling their contents, choosing our footsteps carefully and becoming defensive or overly cautious if anyone gets too close. When they are empty, they are of course lighter and far easier to carry, but we are always looking to fill them up again.

As indicated earlier, my 'water jar' was the filter of 'victimhood' that I chose to look at life through following Andrew's death. I made choices based on the perspective it offered. The contents of my jar were anger, pain and coping strategies. It was a heavy jar, a very full jar and one that took a lot of effort to carry.

The day I encountered Jesus in that meeting was the day I dropped my jar. I let it smash into a thousand pieces and in doing so my filter fell off. I had reached the mountain top and I could see ahead of me. Of course I could see behind me too, but it was not all I could see. I felt hope.

The evening after my encounter with Jesus, I couldn't wait for the evening meeting. I couldn't wait to embrace those whom I had seen as my judge and jury for so long but now I saw as my friends. I got ready for that service, looking in a tiny toilet mirror, and for the first time in eight years I saw beauty and worth. I felt light. I hadn't changed in my personality, because this is who I am and Jesus loves me as I am. I felt God's kiss on my cheek as I walked to the meeting. I felt him whisper, 'I am so proud of you.'

I walked with shoulders back, head held high and joy in my heart. I knew there was a journey ahead, but I knew I wasn't alone. I knew that losing Andrew mattered, but it did not define me anymore. The service began and I walked boldly down the aisle to the front because the music had started and there was only one place I wanted to be. I danced, and I danced, and I danced in a newly found freedom. I danced as if no one was watching. I danced with the angels.

I am not at all suggesting that healing will bring a need to dance at the front of church. I have not since demonstrated such a zealous enthusiasm and I am certainly not about to run to the front and dance again, but I had made my peace with my Saviour whom I had shunned for so long. This was a statement—come and see what the Lord has done. I wanted to praise him, to thank him, but most of all to celebrate with him.

My faith in Jesus had allowed me to let go. Letting go of the question 'Why me?' that had burdened me for eight long years meant that I could let go of low self-esteem. To let go of the anger meant that my perspective about people and God was no longer being poisoned and I was now able to start my own journey with him, accepting myself for who I am and knowing that he does too. Letting go of the shame of my choices that had been my strategies for years meant that I was able to start making choices that helped me to be free.

> *Many of the Samaritans from that town*
> *believed in him because of the woman's*
> *testimony.*
>
> *(John 4:39)*

When the time is right, will you allow yourself to let go and to breathe again? Will you allow yourself to step out of the cave and walk towards the mountain top? Will you hand him your cross? Jesus can make it purposeful.

And for you, the friends of those who are dealing with trauma, may I humbly encourage you to walk with them, to take the cross for them when you can, to carry them and to bear with them in their suffering?

> *I have loved you with an everlasting love;*
> *therefore I have continued my faithfulness*
> *to you.*
>
> *(Jeremiah 31:3, ESV)*

Recommended further reading

Neil T. Anderson, Hal Baumchen,
Finding Hope Again (Regal Books, 1999),
ISBN 978-0-83072-356-0

William Paul Young, *The Shack: Healing for Your
Journey Through Loss, Trauma, and Pain*

John Eldredge, Stasi Eldredge,
Captivating (Thomas Nelson, 2010),
ISBN 978-1-40020-282-9

Julian Evans, Ben Evans, Phil West, Clive Anderson,
A Help in Grief (Day One, 2019),
ISBN 978-1-84625-634-9

Neil T. Anderson,
The Bondage Breaker (Harvest House, 2006),
ISBN 978-0-73691-814-5